Fuck, Now There Are Two of You

by Adam Mansbach

illustrated by Owen Brozman

Published by Akashic Books
Words ©2019 Adam Mansbach
Illustrations ©2019 Owen Brozman

ISBN-13: 978-1-61775-760-0
First printing
Printed in Malaysia

Akashic Books
Brooklyn, New York, USA
Ballydehob, Co. Cork, Ireland
Twitter: @AkashicBooks
Facebook: AkashicBooks
E-mail: info@akashicbooks.com
Website: www.akashicbooks.com

Adam Mansbach is an award-winning novelist, humorist, and screenwriter whose works include the novels *Rage Is Back, Angry Black White Boy*, and *The End of the Jews*, the screenplay for the Netflix Original film *Barry*, and, most recently—with Dave Barry and Alan Zweibel—*A Field Guide to the Jewish People*. He actually has *three* children, two of whom are under two years old. Please send help.

www.AdamMansbach.com

Owen Brozman is an illustrator whose work includes comics, advertisements, murals, album covers, magazines, and more. He illustrated the cookbook *Kindness & Salt*, the graphic novel *Nature of the Beast*, and the previous entry in this series, *You Have to Fucking Eat*. He has worked with Scholastic, *Entertainment Weekly, Time Out New York*, and numerous other clients. He lives with his family in Brooklyn, New York.

www.OwenBrozman.com

For Zanthe and Asa, and Olivia

I have wonderful news for you, darling.
A little brother or sister is coming—what fun!
As for me, my life's pretty much fucked now
Because two's a million more kids than one.

The baby is growing inside Mama's tummy.
Put your hand there—you might feel a kick!
Soon you won't be the focus of all our attention.
Chances are, that will make you a dick.

I never knew love before you came
And I swore that one kid would be it, so
This is a big change for us all, hon.
Our life is one gigantic shit show.

Once there were pockets of quiet
When Mama and Papa could do a few
Grown-up-type things, but not anymore.
Fuck! Now there are two of you.

No, I can't play right now, kiddo.
The babe spent the whole night awake.
I know you feel sad and neglected
But cut me some slack, for fuck's sake.

Wow, so now you're an infant again?
You're watching the baby and following suit?
I don't know how to break this to you, love,
But that shit is not fucking cute.

Looking back, with just you it was easy
To do stuff without a big uproar.
Now the simplest outing's a grueling ordeal.
What the fuck did we sign ourselves up for?

You're so loving and sweet with the baby,
Snuggled in bed, side by side.
It makes me wish I could forget your attempts
At motherfucking fratricide.

Someday you'll entertain one another
While we chill and catch up on our reading.
But for years—fucking years!—there will not be a time
No one's shitting or crying or peeing.

I don't love you any less now, my dear.
Love's not a pie; we don't have to divide it.
I'm just so frazzled I hate everybody
And I'm too fucking tired to hide it.

Sorry, sweetheart, we can't go to the playground.
The baby's so big now—it's tricky to manage her!
And I'll be damned if I let myself be
Outnumbered like some fucking amateur.

The floor and all four walls are covered
In vegetables, pasta, and fruit.
I can vaguely remember when meals did not
require fucking hazmat suits.

Sometimes when you both are sleeping,
We watch you, secure in the knowledge
That one day this madness will come to an end
And you'll both go the fuck off to college.

At two in the morning it hits me.
My heart thumps a-rat-a-tat-tat.
If you two are going to college
How the fuck are we paying for that?

The End